Original title:
The Compassionate Companion

Copyright © 2024 Swan Charm
All rights reserved.

Author: Eliora Lumiste
ISBN HARDBACK: 978-9916-86-608-5
ISBN PAPERBACK: 978-9916-86-609-2
ISBN EBOOK: 978-9916-86-610-8

Hands that Heal

Gentle touch upon the skin,
Whispers of a love within.
With every pat, a balm of grace,
In their warmth, find solace space.

With calloused palms and tender heart,
They bind the wounds, mend every part.
In quiet moments, strength revealed,
In every gesture, hands that heal.

A Tapestry of Care

Stitches woven, thread of gold,
Every knot, a story told.
In vibrant hues, hearts intertwine,
A tapestry of love, divine.

Each piece a token, gently shared,
Of dreams fulfilled and burdens bared.
In every fold, compassion sown,
Together in this warmth, we've grown.

Healing Melodies

Notes that linger in the air,
Softly woven, filled with care.
In harmony, we find our way,
Melodies that heal and stay.

Voices rise in sweet refrain,
Uplifting spirits, easing pain.
With every chord, a story spun,
Together, hearts beat as one.

In the Shade of Compassion

Beneath the boughs, we find our rest,
In kindness shared, we are blessed.
Leaves whisper stories in the breeze,
Of open hearts that seek to please.

In shadows, love is freely given,
A shelter strong, where hope is risen.
With every act of gentle sway,
We bloom anew in light of day.

Where Hearts Reside

In the quiet of the night,
Whispers of love take flight.
Among the stars, they glide,
In this place, hearts reside.

Through storms, we find our way,
Hand in hand, come what may.
In laughter and in tears,
Strength is born through the years.

A gentle touch of grace,
In this warm, sacred space.
Memories softly entwined,
In our hearts, peace we find.

The echoes of the past,
Stitching moments that will last.
Every heartbeat speaks true,
In this haven, me and you.

With love, our spirits soar,
Forever, we explore.
In the light of the moon's pride,
This is where hearts reside.

Constellations of Comfort

In the night sky's embrace,
We find solace and grace.
Stars whisper ancient tales,
Guiding us through life's gales.

In the stillness, hope ignites,
Dreams take flight on starry nights.
Holding hands, we share the spark,
Illuminating the dark.

Each twinkle a gentle touch,
Reminding us we are loved so much.
With each constellation's glow,
A tapestry of feelings flow.

Through the cosmos, hearts align,
A dance of fate, so divine.
We trace the lines of our desires,
Fanning the flames of inner fires.

In this universe of delight,
Together, we'll face the night.
For in the stars, we discover,
Constellations of one another.

A Garden of Empathy

In the heart of the morn,
Blooms of kindness are born.
With petals soft and bright,
They reach for the warm light.

Each flower tells a story,
Of pain, hope, and glory.
Beneath the sun's embrace,
We find our rightful place.

In the soil, love takes root,
Nurtured by the tender shoot.
With every drop of rain,
We nurture joy through pain.

The fragrance of understanding,
A breeze, ever expanding.
In this garden, we share,
Compassion blooms everywhere.

Among the greens, our laughter,
We cultivate ever after.
In this sacred space, we see,
A garden of empathy.

Illuminated Paths

On the winding road we tread,
With dreams and hopes we're led.
Each step is a gentle song,
Guiding us where we belong.

Beneath the stars, we wander,
In silence, hearts grow fonder.
Guided by the moon's soft gleam,
Together, we chase the dream.

With every twist and turn,
New lessons we shall learn.
Light the way with trust and care,
In this journey, love we share.

Through shadows and through light,
We'll embrace every fright.
Hand in hand, we'll navigate,
Fate and love will celebrate.

With courage, we'll ascend,
On the paths that never end.
In every step, we find our way,
Illuminated paths we lay.

Embracing Every Moment

In the dawn's soft light, we rise anew,
Every heartbeat whispers, life is true.
Moments fleeting, like petals blown,
In each breath, a story sewn.

Gather the laughter, hold it near,
In joyful echoes, cast out fear.
Every smile, a spark of grace,
A fleeting dance in time and space.

The sunset paints the sky in hues,
Reminding us of paths we choose.
In every shadow, light will creep,
Embrace the magic, dive in deep.

With open hearts and arms stretched wide,
We journey forth, no need to hide.
Each second counts, a treasure found,
In love's embrace, we are unbound.

So here's to living, bright and bold,
In every moment, let love unfold.
For life's a gift, a fleeting song,
In every heartbeat, we belong.

Fireside Reflections

The crackling fire, a warm embrace,
It dances softly, a fleeting trace.
In the glow, we find our peace,
As the world outside begins to cease.

With thoughts like embers, memories flare,
Stories whispered, filled with care.
Each recollection, a thread we weave,
In the calm of night, we truly believe.

The flicker of flames, a timeless guide,
Inviting us to set aside pride.
In this moment, we gather near,
Sharing our dreams, our hopes sincere.

Old songs echo through the night air,
Carried on whispers, tales we share.
In laughter's warmth, we find our light,
Illuminating shadows, chasing the night.

As hearthstone glows, we close our eyes,
Lost in the rhythm, where comfort lies.
In every crackle, a memory born,
Fireside reflections, hearts reborn.

Tomorrow awaits, with its dawn so bright,
Yet here we linger, in this sacred light.
For within this moment, we're forever whole,
Fireside reflections, warming the soul.

Embracing Solitude

In quiet corners of my mind,
Peace unfolds like morning light.
Shadows dance, but I am fine,
In solitude, my heart takes flight.

Nature whispers soft and low,
Breezes carry tales untold.
In silence, inner gardens grow,
A sanctuary to behold.

Each moment deepens my embrace,
With every breath, I find my way.
Alone, I find my sacred space,
In solitude, I learn to play.

No echo of the outside world,
Just the heartbeat of my soul.
In stillness, dreams slowly unfurled,
In solitude, I am whole.

Familiar Strangers

In crowded rooms, we meet and part,
Yet there's warmth in fleeting eyes.
Connections bloom within the heart,
Familiar strangers, silent ties.

A smile shared across the way,
Words unspoken, yet profound.
In moments lost, we tend to stay,
A thread of grace that knows no bounds.

Each glance a bridge, each nod a spark,
In passing lives, we find our place.
Together woven in the dark,
Familiar strangers, full of grace.

With every chance encounter's hue,
New stories whisper through the air.
In vibrant worlds, we start anew,
Each stranger holds a bond to share.

Guardians of Grace

Amidst the chaos, we stand tall,
Hearts aglow with purest light.
With every struggle, we won't fall,
Guardians of grace, we unite.

Each act of kindness, like a seed,
Planted in the souls we touch.
In this world, we choose to lead,
A gentle force that means so much.

Through storms of life, we serve and care,
A healing hand, a listening ear.
Together, burdens we must share,
Guardians of grace, drawing near.

With open hearts, we pave the way,
For love to flourish, dreams to soar.
In every moment, come what may,
We stand as guardians, evermore.

The Heart's Harmony

In melodies where silence lives,
The heart beats steady, true and warm.
With every note, a story gives,
In harmony, we find our form.

Each whisper of a gentle breeze,
Carries souls, entwined like song.
In nature's tune, we find our ease,
A symphony where we belong.

Through every trial, each dissonance,
The heart finds ways to weave anew.
With patience, love creates a dance,
A harmony that pulls us through.

In twinkling stars, in rustling leaves,
The rhythm of our lives takes flight.
A song of hope the spirit weaves,
In every moment, pure delight.

Colors of Compassion

In hues of warmth and gentle grace,
We find the kindness we embrace.
A touch of love in every shade,
Compassion blooms, never to fade.

With every heart that learns to care,
Colors blend, a vibrant air.
Through storms of life, we'll paint anew,
A canvas bright with every hue.

The pastel whispers of a friend,
Soft gestures shared, they never end.
In grays and blues, we find our way,
Together stronger, come what may.

In golden light, we share our hope,
An endless stretch, a wider scope.
Each stroke of grace, a bridge we build,
Love's palette shines, our hearts fulfilled.

Through colors rich and stories shared,
Compassion's song, forever bared.
Hand in hand, we journey on,
In the spectrum's glow, we will respond.

Guardian of Dreams

In twilight hours, I stand so still,
A watchful soul, a whispered thrill.
Beneath the stars, I softly tread,
To guard the dreams that dance in bed.

With gentle sighs, I weave the night,
Creating worlds of pure delight.
Each wish unfurls, a tale to tell,
In slumber's arms, all is well.

A lantern's glow, a guiding star,
I hold the hopes, both near and far.
Through velvet skies, I spread my wings,
To cradle dreams like precious things.

With every heartbeat, I promise still,
To watch and guard, to guide with will.
In realms of fantasy, I find my place,
A guardian's love, a warm embrace.

When dawn arrives, I'll fade away,
But in your heart, I long to stay.
A memory of the stars that gleam,
A promise kept—the guardian of dreams.

The Fabric of Togetherness

Woven tightly, thread by thread,
In every laugh, in tears we've shed.
A tapestry of hearts entwined,
In bonds of love, our souls aligned.

Each moment shared, a stitch we make,
Through every joy and every ache.
In colors rich of life's embrace,
Together we find our sacred space.

From distant shores, we find our way,
In unity, our spirits sway.
Across the miles, our hearts remain,
Connected through the joy and pain.

The fabric holds each memory dear,
With every thread, we conquer fear.
In every hug, a comfort found,
A quilt of love, forever bound.

Through storms and sunny skies above,
We gather strength in endless love.
The fabric speaks, in whispers clear,
Togetherness—a bond sincere.

Stars in Your Eyes

In quiet nights, I see the glow,
Of countless dreams, a cosmic flow.
Your eyes reflect the worlds unknown,
A universe where love has grown.

Each sparkle holds a hidden wish,
In stardust trails, a secret fish.
With wonder vast, they softly shine,
In depths profound, our hearts entwine.

When shadows fall, your eyes ignite,
A beacon bright, a guiding light.
Through darkest paths, they lead the way,
In every glance, the night turns day.

With galaxies that whisper dreams,
Your gaze unveils what truly beams.
Every sparkle tells a tale,
Of journeys rich, together sail.

In every twinkle, I find my place,
A love that blooms in time and space.
With stars in your eyes, I see my truth,
An endless dance of ageless youth.

Walking Together in Silence

In gardens lush where whispers dwell,
Two souls collide, a tale to tell.
With every step, the silence breathes,
Connecting hearts as nature weaves.

Through rustling leaves and gentle skies,
We speak in looks, no need for lies.
The world fades away, a soft embrace,
In this stillness, we find our place.

The sun dips low, the shadows span,
Hand in hand, we understand.
A quiet peace, our spirits soar,
Together, we crave, we seek for more.

With every dawn, new paths await,
In silence shared, we dance with fate.
In every heartbeat, stories shared,
For in this hush, our souls are bared.

Forevermore in twilight's glow,
Together through highs and softly low.
In silence wrapped, we voyage far,
Two wanderers beneath the star.

When Shadows Fall

When shadows fall and daylight fades,
A whispering dusk, the evening wades.
The world transforms as colors blur,
In twilight's arms, lost dreams occur.

The chilling breeze, a quiet sigh,
Leaves dance in silence, gently lie.
The stars emerge, a twinkling treat,
As night draws close, we feel the beat.

In hidden corners, secrets dwell,
Stories long forgotten swell.
The moon, a beacon, softly calls,
To lovers' hearts, where magic thralls.

With every shadow, a tale retold,
Of fleeting moments, memories bold.
In darkness deep, hope finds its way,
As shadows play, we learn to stay.

For when the light begins to hide,
In shadows cast, we must abide.
Through every night, though fears may crawl,
We rise again when shadows fall.

In the Depths of Solitude

In the depths of solitude we find,
A quiet peace, a tranquil mind.
The world outside fades into grey,
As thoughts unwind and gently sway.

The echoing silence, solace sweet,
Each breath a rhythm, each heartbeat.
In stillness, clarity arises,
Truth beneath the chaos disguises.

Yet in this space, a spark ignites,
Solitude births the truest sights.
Where shadows dance and light takes form,
We find our strength amidst the norm.

Through the dark, the light shines clear,
In quiet corners, dreams appear.
With open hearts, the world unfolds,
A journey rich with tales untold.

In solitude's embrace, we grow,
In the silence, wisdom flows.
For in the depths, we learn to see,
The beauty found in being free.

A Harvest of Compassion

In fields of kindness, hearts will yield,
A harvest rich, a bounteous field.
With open hands, we sow each seed,
Of love and care, of every need.

Compassion blooms where kindness grows,
In every act, a soft wind blows.
From heart to heart, the echoes ring,
A symphony of hope we bring.

In storms of doubt, we stand as one,
Together brave until we're done.
Through trials faced, through tears we share,
A tapestry of love laid bare.

From whispered thoughts to actions bold,
Compassion's warmth will break the cold.
With every gesture, light will reign,
In hearts united, peace will gain.

A harvest gathered, strong and vast,
In every moment, love will last.
For when we care and lend a hand,
We sow the seeds to heal the land.

A Touch of Grace

In a world so fast and loud,
Gentle whispers gather round.
Softest hands that heal the ache,
In the quiet, hearts awake.

Moments woven, pure delight,
Glistening like stars at night.
With each touch, a spark ignites,
Carving pathways to new heights.

Grace unveils the hidden light,
Guides the lost with tender might.
In the shadows, hope will trace,
Every soul a warm embrace.

Beneath the weight of worldly cares,
A loving calm, a breath that shares.
In the dance of fate we blend,
With grace and love, the heart will mend.

Navigator of Stormy Seas

Beneath the dark and raging skies,
A heart beats true, no need for lies.
With steady hands upon the wheel,
It charts the course, unyielding, real.

Waves may crash and storms may roar,
But strength will rise forevermore.
Through tempests wild and trials deep,
A promise made, a bond to keep.

Stars above, a guiding light,
Navigating through the night.
Trust the journey, trust the soul,
For every challenge makes us whole.

In the heart of every gale,
The spirit stands, it will not fail.
With courage as the steadfast creed,
We sail on, we will succeed.

The Silent Strength

In silence dwells a power vast,
A still resolve that holds steadfast.
Through whispered winds and gentle sighs,
It rises strong, beneath the skies.

Like ancient trees that bend but don't break,
Through every storm, they seldom shake.
Roots run deep, unyielding grace,
In every struggle, find your place.

Moments shared in quiet time,
Strength of spirit, tall as a rhyme.
In unity, we find our way,
Silent strength will guide our stay.

With every tear and every laugh,
We'll carve our path, a lasting craft.
In the stillness, we shall see,
The strength within, eternally.

A Soft Place to Fall

When the world is harsh and cold,
And the weight becomes too bold,
Seek the space where love abides,
A haven found, where hope resides.

In gentle arms, the heart can rest,
Safe from trials, a tranquil nest.
Life's tumult fades, the storm drifts away,
Wrapped in warmth, we choose to stay.

A soft place built on trust and grace,
Where every dream can find its space.
Together we shall mend the seams,
In the quiet, we'll weave our dreams.

With every laugh and every tear,
We find solace, far and near.
In love's embrace, we learn to stand,
A soft place, hand in hand.

Moments of Grace

In the hush of dawn's first light,
Whispers of joy take gentle flight.
A touch of warmth, a fleeting glance,
In stillness found, we seek our chance.

Each leaf that falls, a story shared,
In silent woods, our hearts declared.
Nature's breath cradles our pain,
Moments of grace in early rain.

Glimmers of hope in shadows cast,
Fragments of dreams, we hold them fast.
As time flows by, we learn to see,
Life's tender gifts, our hearts set free.

With every sigh and thankful prayer,
We weave sweet blessings everywhere.
In laughter's tune and sorrow's song,
These moments of grace keep us strong.

In the Company of Hope

When skies are grey and doubt looms near,
We gather strength, dispel our fear.
In every heart, a spark remains,
In the company of hope we gain.

Through winding paths, our spirits rise,
With steadfast hearts, we touch the skies.
In stories shared, through joy and pain,
The bonds of hope we will sustain.

Each candle lit in darkest nights,
Guides us towards those shining lights.
Together we stand, hand in hand,
In the company of hope, we'll stand.

From ashes born, we blaze anew,
Embracing life in hues of blue.
With open arms and open minds,
In the company of hope, love finds.

The Silent Guardian

Beneath the stars, a shadow looms,
In quiet grace, the heart consumes.
A watchful gaze, both strong and kind,
The silent guardian stands behind.

With every tear and whispered sigh,
They carry dreams, we know they fly.
In every storm, they are the light,
A beacon shining through the night.

Through whispered winds and rustling leaves,
Their presence felt, our soul believes.
In silent moments, we find rest,
The silent guardian knows us best.

A gentle hand in time of need,
Guiding us through, our hearts they lead.
With every step, a trust expands,
The silent guardian understands.

Days of Shared Dreams

In golden light, our visions merge,
With laughter's lift, our hopes converge.
Moments stitched with silver thread,
In the tapestry of dreams we've spread.

Whispers of futures yet to unfold,
Together we weave, our stories bold.
With courageous hearts, we chase the dawn,
In days of shared dreams, love is drawn.

Through valleys deep, on mountains high,
With open eyes, we touch the sky.
In unity found, we are complete,
In days of shared dreams, life is sweet.

Every heartbeat, a song we sing,
In joy and sorrow, we take wing.
Hand in hand, through the endless seams,
We cherish our days of shared dreams.

The Unseen Hand

In shadows where whispers dwell,
A touch that guides us near,
Through silence, we find our way,
A heart's soft voice to hear.

Moments lost, yet never gone,
Threads of fate tightly spun,
In every choice, every bond,
Our journey has begun.

Invisible forces at play,
Woven through time and space,
Though unseen, their power grows,
In every warm embrace.

With every step, we learn to trust,
This hand, though never shown,
Will guide us through the stormy nights,
And lead us safely home.

So let us walk with open hearts,
In faith, we build our stand,
Embracing all the unseen grace,
Of love's own gentle hand.

Together in Stillness

Beneath the vast and starry sky,
We find our refuge here,
In quiet moments shared with you,
Our worries disappear.

The world outside may rush and roar,
But in your gaze, I stay,
Together in the stillness,
We find a brighter way.

With every breath, we harmonize,
In rhythm, hearts align,
Though time may falter in its pace,
Forever, you are mine.

In silence, whispers resonate,
Of dreams we've yet to chase,
With hands entwined, we move as one,
In this tranquil space.

So let us linger in this calm,
Where love, like rivers, flow,
Together in our stillness,
We nurture what we sow.

Threads of Empathy

Woven into every heart,
A tapestry so fine,
In stories shared and burdens borne,
We touch the Divine.

With every thread, a tale unfolds,
Of joy and sorrow's song,
In understanding's gentle grasp,
Together, we belong.

Through eyes that see beyond the veil,
We bridge the distance wide,
In each other's pain and triumph,
We take the path of pride.

Empathy is a guiding light,
That leads us through the night,
In every heart, a story waits,
To bring our souls to light.

So let us weave the threads of hope,
In kindness, we shall stand,
For in the fabric of our lives,
We're stitched by love's own hand.

The Warmth of Shared Burdens

Upon the road of heavy days,
We carry weights unseen,
But in the strength of unity,
Our spirits find a sheen.

When shadows dance on weary backs,
And troubles feel too vast,
We lift each other's heavy hearts,
And weave a bond to last.

Through trials faced and tears we've shed,
We find a deeper grace,
In sharing loads and lifting hope,
We carve a brighter place.

For burdens shared are joys combined,
And laughter lights the load,
With every step, hand in hand,
We journey down this road.

So let us cherish every weight,
That helps our souls to grow,
In the warmth of shared burdens,
Together, we will glow.

Tender Echoes of Understanding

In whispers soft, we find the way,
Where shadows dance and colors play.
Each sigh a bridge, each smile a thread,
In silent vows, our hearts are fed.

Beneath the stars, we share our dreams,
In gentle winds, our laughter gleams.
With every glance, the world aligns,
In tender echoes, love entwines.

Through storms and trials, hand in hand,
A fortress built on shifting sand.
With patience worn like woven lace,
We forge a bond, a sacred space.

In moments brief, we linger still,
With open hearts, we seek to heal.
The threads of time, they softly weave,
In every sigh, we choose to believe.

Together we rise, through joy and pain,
In sweet remembrance, we'll sustain.
For in each echo, truth does bloom,
With understanding, we share the room.

Between Heartbeats

A pause, a silence, a fleeting glance,
In the space where heartbeats dance.
Moments hold worlds, so close, yet far,
In every whisper, a guiding star.

Time blurs in the warmth of your gaze,
Caught in the soft, golden haze.
The rhythm of life, so sweet, so rare,
In our unspoken thoughts, we share.

Between the beats, a story flows,
A gentle pulse, where true love grows.
In perfect sync, our souls align,
An endless loop, a sacred sign.

Each heartbeat holds a promise made,
In silent vows, our fears allayed.
For between heartbeats, we intertwine,
In tender moments, souls combine.

The clock may tick, but we stand still,
In this embrace, our hearts fulfill.
Together in rhythm, forever we'll stay,
In the silence between, love finds its way.

Bonds Unseen

A glance exchanged, a subtle nod,
In hidden ways, we find the broad.
Through unspoken ties, we come to know,
The bond that deepens, like rivers flow.

In laughter shared, in tears long shed,
A silent language, softly said.
With every word that's left unspoken,
In gentle hearts, the promise woken.

Across the miles, like threads of gold,
In memories cherished, stories told.
Though distance may stretch, love remains near,
In every heart, the warmth we steer.

In shadows cast, we find our light,
Embraced by hope, a future bright.
Though ties might seem so faint, so thin,
Within the depths, the love begins.

Bonds unseen, yet deeply felt,
In every wound, a warmth dealt.
Together we weave a tapestry,
In threads of love, we will always be.

The Language of Kindness

In simple gestures, words unspoken,
A smile shared, a heart awoken.
The warmth of touch, a hand to hold,
In kindness wrapped, our stories unfold.

Like gentle rain on thirsty land,
Compassion flows, a guiding hand.
In every act, a seed we sow,
A world transformed, where kindness grows.

In patient ears that truly listen,
With open hearts, our spirits glisten.
Through every challenge, we stand brave,
In the language of kindness, love will pave.

A flicker bright in darkest hour,
In smallest deeds, we find our power.
With words of comfort, we uplift,
In kindness shared, the greatest gift.

Together we rise, through thick and thin,
In every loss, a chance to begin.
For in this language, so pure, so free,
We find the path to harmony.

Hearts Aligned

In the quiet of the night,
Two souls meet in gentle light.
Fingers brush, a silent spark,
In their gaze, they leave their mark.

With every heartbeat, they draw near,
Words unspoken, yet so clear.
Mirrored dreams in starlit skies,
Together, they will rise.

Paths entwined, a dance of fate,
In this love, they celebrate.
Moments flow like rivers wide,
In each other, they confide.

Through the storms, they stand as one,
Facing battles until they're done.
With shared hope, they navigate,
Hearts aligned, they create.

In the warmth of morning sun,
They find strength as they run.
Side by side, no need to roam,
In each other, they are home.

A Labyrinth of Understanding

In the maze of thought and care,
We wander through layers rare.
Each twist reveals another sign,
A dance of hearts, a bond divine.

Through shadows cast by doubt, we tread,
Seeking truth in what is said.
In silence, we closely feel,
The delicate threads that weave and heal.

Voices soft, yet filled with might,
Guide us further into the light.
With every step, bridges form,
In our embrace, we are warm.

Through the depth of night's embrace,
We discover a sacred space.
In the labyrinth, we prevail,
Learning love will not derail.

At journeys' end, we find our way,
In this bond, come what may.
With open hearts, hand in hand,
Together, we will always stand.

Beyond the Noise

Amidst the chaos, we find peace,
Where worries pause, and troubles cease.
In the stillness, we hear a song,
A melody that sings us along.

Voices fade, distractions slip,
As we steady our shared grip.
Calm reflections, whispers clear,
In every moment, you are near.

Through the clamor of the day,
Our hearts converse in gentle sway.
In this space where time stands still,
Each heartbeat echoes love's sweet thrill.

We rise above the rushing tide,
In the silence, we confide.
Here we find our sacred ground,
In this love, true strength is found.

Beyond the noise, where magic lies,
In your gaze, the world complies.
Together, we paint the skies,
With colors born from love's replies.

Whispers of Hope

In the dawn of a brand-new day,
Hope arises in gentle sway.
With every breath, we ignite the fire,
Chasing dreams that lift us higher.

Through the valleys, shadows may cast,
Yet in our hearts, the spark will last.
With every step, we choose to rise,
Guided by love, we claim the skies.

In quiet moments, we will find,
The strength that lives within our mind.
In whispered tales, we sow the seeds,
Of courage borne from tender deeds.

As the night gives way to dawn,
Together, we will carry on.
With hands entwined, we'll dare to dream,
In hope's embrace, we find our theme.

For in the whispers, futures gleam,
Through every joy, through every beam.
In this journey, hearts will cope,
United, we are whispers of hope.

Walking Alongside

In the morning light we stroll,
Side by side, both heart and soul.
Whispers carried on the breeze,
Nature's voice, our minds at ease.

Footsteps dance on winding trails,
With each turn, a story hails.
The path unfolds like a dream,
Together, stronger together we beam.

Leaves above tickle our heads,
As sun casts gold on grassy beds.
Laughter echoes in the air,
Moments cherished, sweet and rare.

Through quiet woods, to rivers wide,
In this journey, we confide.
Every shadow, every light,
Walking alongside, pure delight.

As day yields to twilight's grace,
We find peace in our embrace.
Hand in hand, we journey on,
In love's glow, forever drawn.

Kindred Spirits in the Night

Stars flicker in the velvet sky,
Two souls meet with a knowing sigh.
Underneath the moon's soft glow,
Whispers shared, love starts to grow.

Silent wishes float on air,
Understanding, deep and rare.
In the quiet, hearts collide,
Kindred spirits, side by side.

The night blooms with dreams untold,
In this warmth, we find our bold.
Every glance, a silent vow,
Carved in time, the here and now.

As constellations spin above,
We weave a tapestry of love.
Every heartbeat synchronized,
In this moment, mesmerized.

Together we embrace the stars,
No distance can break our bars.
In the beauty of the night,
Kindred spirits, shining bright.

Refuge from the Storm

Raindrops tap against the pane,
In this shelter, we remain.
The howling wind sings its song,
Here, together, we belong.

Thunder rumbles, nature's roar,
You and I, we seek for more.
Wrapped in warmth, we find our peace,
In each other, worries cease.

Clouds may darken, shadows cast,
But our love will ever last.
In this haven from the night,
We find solace, pure delight.

Through the tempest, we will stand,
Holding tight, hand in hand.
For what matters, we embrace,
In the storm, we find our place.

Raindrops may fall, skies may moan,
Together, we are never alone.
In this refuge, hearts transform,
A love that thrives, a perfect storm.

The Heart's Haven

In the quiet glow of dawn,
A gentle place, where dreams are drawn.
The heart whispers a sweet tune,
In this haven, beneath the moon.

With every breath, a story flows,
In the stillness, love bestows.
Each heartbeat, a sacred rhyme,
Moment captured, lost in time.

Warmed by laughter, shared delight,
In this space, we take our flight.
Every secret, soft and true,
In the heart's haven, me and you.

Through the storms and sunny days,
In this haven, love displays.
Sheltered under our embrace,
Together, we have found our place.

As our journey intertwines,
In each moment, our love shines.
A treasure held, forever known,
In the heart's haven, we have grown.

Whispers of Warmth

In the quiet of the night,
Soft voices shimmer and ignite,
Gentle breezes brush the skin,
In this moment, warmth begins.

Stars above in velvet skies,
Guide us where our spirit flies,
A whispered promise, sweet and clear,
In this bond, we conquer fear.

The world may spin and swirl around,
Yet here, it's safe, our souls profound,
Embracing light, we walk as one,
Together till the rising sun.

Fires crackle, stories shared,
In each gaze, a heart laid bare,
With every laugh and every sigh,
We weave our dreams, we learn to fly.

So let the winter winds blow cold,
In our hearts, love's warmth is bold,
Hand in hand, we face it all,
Together strong, we will not fall.

Together in Shadows

In twilight's hush, beneath the trees,
Where shadows dance and hearts find ease,
We walk the path of dusk and dawn,
In silent whispers, dreams are drawn.

Our laughter echoes through the night,
Wrapped in a cloak of soft moonlight,
Every secret shared in trust,
Together, rise we surely must.

Fingers intertwine, a gentle clasp,
In solitude, our spirits grasp,
Though the world may turn away,
In shadows deep, we choose to stay.

Through battles fought and tears that flow,
In quiet strength, our love will grow,
For in the dark, we find our way,
Together bold, come what may.

So let the stars bear witness bright,
To hearts entwined in love's pure light,
In shadows deep, we create our song,
Together, forever, where we belong.

Embrace of Understanding

In silent glances, truths unfold,
A language deeper than words told,
In every pause, a shared refrain,
An embrace where warmth will reign.

With open hearts, we learn to see,
The fragile threads that weave you and me,
Every story holds a spark,
In understanding, we leave our mark.

Through trials faced and dreams unveiled,
In each other's arms, we have sailed,
Navigating storms, we find our peace,
In the quiet, our fears release.

Moments linger, breaths align,
Time slows down, your hand in mine,
With gentle patience, we redefine,
In every heartbeat, love's design.

So let the world keep rushing past,
In this embrace, our love will last,
Bound by understanding, strong and true,
Together forever, just me and you.

Tides of Tenderness

Soft waves crash upon the shore,
Whispers of love, forevermore,
Every tide brings us closer still,
In gentle laps, it's love we fill.

With every ebb, we learn to trust,
In soft caress, it's more than lust,
For in this rhythm, hearts align,
Together dancing, pure divine.

As moonlight bathes the tranquil sea,
Your eyes reflect the depth of me,
In tender moments, we both know,
Together, like the tides, we flow.

Every sunrise paints the sky,
With colors bright, our spirits fly,
Through every high and every low,
In tenderness, our love will grow.

So here we stand, as one we rise,
With whispered dreams and soft replies,
In the depths of love's embrace,
Together we find our rightful place.

Through the Lens of Care

In quiet whispers, love does bloom,
A tender glance, dispelling gloom.
Moments shared, as seasons change,
Through every shadow, hearts rearrange.

With open arms, we face the dawn,
In shared laughter, we carry on.
Gentle touch, a soothing balm,
In chaos, find a sacred calm.

Through thick and thin, we stand as one,
Together shining, like the sun.
With every tear, a story told,
In kindness, hearts will never fold.

Embracing flaws, we learn and grow,
In every triumph, let love glow.
Through storms we weather, hand in hand,
In unity, forever we stand.

The Power of a Handhold

Fingers entwined, a whispered trust,
In silent moments, we adjust.
A simple clasp, yet worlds collide,
In shared warmth, hearts open wide.

Through trials faced, we take our stand,
A lifeline formed, in love so grand.
Each heartbeat echoes, side by side,
In every challenge, we confide.

With gentle strength, we steer through night,
Hand in hand, we find the light.
No words needed, just your squeeze,
In this union, my heart's at ease.

In crowded rooms, or spaces bare,
Your touch reminds me, love is rare.
With every step, we brave the path,
Through joy and sorrow, we share the last.

Journeys of the Heart

Wandering souls, we roam the earth,
In search of love, we find our worth.
Across the miles, our spirits soar,
In every heartbeat, we crave more.

Pathways twist, yet fate aligns,
In every smile, our journey shines.
With every step, we learn to see,
The beauty lies in simply being free.

In quiet moments, reflections bloom,
Echoes of laughter fill the room.
Together we chase the fading light,
In shared stories, our hearts take flight.

Through valleys deep and mountains high,
In unity, together we try.
With every mile that we embrace,
We chart the course, find our place.

The Echo of Your Voice

Softly spoken, your words confide,
In each whisper, dreams reside.
Resonating through the night,
Your melody brings pure delight.

A gentle laugh, a soothing song,
In your presence, I feel strong.
With every story, layers unfold,
Crafting memories, rich and bold.

Through peaks and valleys, your voice remains,
A constant thread in life's refrains.
In gripped silence, I hear you clear,
A guiding light, forever near.

As days do pass and seasons turn,
In your echo, my heart will yearn.
For every heartbeat sings your name,
In love's embrace, we are aflame.

A Rainbow After Rain

After the storm, skies clear,
Colors bloom, bright and near.
Nature whispers soft and low,
A promise made, a gentle glow.

Raindrops kiss the earth anew,
Sparkling gems in morning dew.
Each hue tells a story bright,
Hope restored in the warm light.

Clouds retreat, the sun does shine,
A canvas vast, the colors twine.
With every shade, a tale unfolds,
A tapestry of dreams retold.

Children laugh and dance around,
With joy in every vibrant sound.
They chase the light, so joyous free,
In this moment, they truly see.

Hold on tight to fleeting dreams,
Like rainbows born from sunlit beams.
For after storms, beauty appears,
A sign of hope throughout the years.

Moments of Clarity

In the hush of the morning light,
Thoughts unclouded, pure delight.
A pause to breathe, to simply be,
In the stillness, I find me.

Golden rays warm the skin,
A chance for growth, to begin.
Life unfolds like petals wide,
Each moment, a truth inside.

Waves of doubt begin to fade,
In clarity, I'm unafraid.
Lessons learned, I stand anew,
Embracing all that I can do.

Time slows down, the mind finds peace,
From restless thoughts, I seek release.
In every heartbeat, wisdom sings,
Awakening the joy it brings.

These moments swift, yet deeply felt,
In their grace, my troubles melt.
With eyes open, I see the way,
Through clarity, I seize the day.

The Quiet Rescuer

Beneath the weight of silent tears,
A heart whispers, facing fears.
In shadows deep, a gentle hand,
A friend appears, just like they planned.

No grand gestures, just a smile,
A tender gaze that goes a mile.
In quiet moments, strength is found,
In words unspoken, solace abound.

When darkness looms and hope feels lost,
The quiet rescuer counts the cost.
They stay present, a steady ground,
In their embrace, peace is profound.

With open arms, the soul finds rest,
In stillness shared, we are our best.
No need for noise or battle cries,
The calm within, where love resides.

In every sigh, a bond flows strong,
The quiet whisper, a heartfelt song.
For in the silence, hearts connect,
In the space between, pure respect.

Lighthouses in the Fog

In the thickened mist, I roam,
Searching for a guiding home.
Lighthouses stand, a beacon bright,
Shining through the veils of night.

Their steady glow, a watchful eye,
Leading lost souls to the sky.
With every beam, a promise made,
To navigate through fear and fade.

In swirling gray, I find my way,
With whispered winds, the spirits sway.
Each lighthouse holds a tale of hope,
An anchor strong, a way to cope.

With patience, time unveils the truth,
In every storm, they offer proof.
When all seems lost, their light remains,
A steadfast guide through life's terrains.

So I walk on, with heart in hand,
Trusting the glow, the soft command.
In fog or storm, I'll find my way,
With lighthouses bright, I'll never stray.

The Art of Listening

In the quiet, words take flight,
Softly spoken, hearts ignite.
Listening close, we find our way,
In silence, thoughts often sway.

Every sigh, a story told,
In the warmth, connections hold.
Weaving dreams with gentle care,
In each moment, we are there.

Ears attuned to whispered fears,
Finding strength through tender tears.
In the pause, a chance to grow,
As understanding starts to flow.

With every heartbeat, we share time,
In the rhythm, a subtle rhyme.
Learning to be, not just to hear,
In the presence, we draw near.

So let us cherish every sound,
In the stillness, love is found.
Through the art, we build a bridge,
In the echo, we won't budge.

Sails of Support

With courage strong, we set the course,
On the waves, we find our force.
Each gust of wind, a helping hand,
Together, we will surely stand.

Through storms that may seek to divide,
Loyal hearts, we will abide.
Like sails that lift in unity,
Bound by hope, we sail the sea.

Anchored firm in trust and care,
In every challenge, we will dare.
Navigating darker skies,
With every storm, we rise and rise.

In laughter's light, we find our way,
Guided by the warmth of day.
Through currents deep, we never tire,
Fueled by love, igniting fire.

As we journey side by side,
In the waves, we will abide.
With sails unfurled, our spirits soar,
Together, we are ever more.

Breath of Comfort

In gentle winds, a soft embrace,
Breathing in the calm of grace.
With every sigh, we let it go,
Finding peace in the ebb and flow.

Wrapped in warmth, a quiet light,
Guiding us through the endless night.
In stillness, we begin to heal,
With breath, our souls learn to feel.

Letting worries drift away,
In this space, we choose to stay.
The rhythm of our hearts aligns,
In every moment, love defines.

So take my hand, let's breathe anew,
In every heartbeat, hope will brew.
Together, deep breaths we will share,
In comfort's arms, we find our care.

With every inhale, we rise above,
In the silence, we find love.
In the breath, a sacred trust,
In comfort's warmth, we must adjust.

In the Depths, a Light

When shadows fall and fears take hold,
In the depths, we find the bold.
A flicker shines, a beacon bright,
Guiding us through the long night.

In the dark, where doubts reside,
A spark of hope, our hearts confide.
With whispers soft, the light will grow,
Leading us to a place we know.

Through winding paths and rocky terrain,
The light remains, despite the pain.
Each step we take, the vision clear,
In the depths, love conquers fear.

So let us journey hand in hand,
In the light, we make our stand.
With every heartbeat, courage grows,
In the depths, the spirit glows.

As dawn will break, the shadows fade,
In the light, new plans are laid.
With open hearts, we'll face the day,
In the depths, we've found our way.

The Gift of Presence

In quiet moments, we find peace,
A warmth that wraps, a sweet release.
Each glance exchanged, a silent vow,
To be together, here and now.

Words unspoken, hearts align,
In simple presence, love will shine.
Through every trial, each heavy sigh,
Together we rise, like birds on high.

The gift of time, a treasured grace,
In laughter shared, we find our place.
Within the chaos, a gentle breath,
In presence we conquer, defying death.

So let us sit, and just be still,
In this moment, we choose goodwill.
Together yet free, our spirits soar,
In the gift of presence, we find more.

Healing Through Connection

In gentle whispers, hearts unite,
In shared fragments, we find light.
Each story told, a bridge we build,
Through connection, our souls are filled.

Hands held tight, with warmth they share,
In every presence, a soothing care.
Through tears and laughter, we gently mend,
Healing grows where hearts extend.

The ties that bind us are strong and true,
In each other's gaze, we see the new.
Like rivers flowing to the sea,
Together we heal, just you and me.

With every heartbeat, we draw near,
In unity's arms, we conquer fear.
Through connection's grace, we lift the veil,
A journey together, we shall prevail.

Sheltering Wings

Beneath the sky, a haven found,
In gentle shelter, love is bound.
Softly, we gather, like feathers in flight,
Under the wings that shield the night.

With whispered prayers, we find our way,
Through storms that come, we choose to stay.
In the clasp of friendship, fears disperse,
With sheltering wings, we break the curse.

Love's warm embrace, a silent cheer,
In fleeting moments, we draw near.
With nurturing hearts, we lift each other,
In the dance of life, we are like a mother.

Through darkened skies, we'll brave the fight,
In every shadow, we'll seek the light.
Together we soar, through highs and lows,
With sheltering wings, our bond just grows.

Navigating the Clouds

In skies of grey, we set our sights,
On distant dreams and glimmering lights.
With courage held, we face the unknown,
In navigating clouds, we've truly grown.

Each twist and turn, a lesson learned,
Through every storm, a fire burned.
With hearts as compasses, we chart the way,
In the dance of life, come what may.

With every challenge, we find our grace,
In the art of flight, we find our place.
Through billowed sails, our spirits ride,
Navigating clouds, we let love guide.

Together we rise, on wings of hope,
Through turbulent skies, we learn to cope.
With laughter and tears, we brave the shroud,
In this shared journey, we're ever proud.

Ever-present Solace

In quiet whispers, hope remains,
A gentle touch through all the pains.
A calm embrace in darkest night,
The heart finds peace, the soul takes flight.

When shadows loom and doubts arise,
A spark of faith beneath the skies.
With every sigh, the spirit clears,
In solace found, we dry our tears.

Through trials faced, we stand as one,
With love's warm light, our battles won.
A steadfast hand, a listening ear,
In endless trust, we conquer fear.

Each moment shared, a treasure pure,
In laughter's echo, hearts endure.
Together bright, our dreams ignite,
With every pulse, we chase the light.

Though storms may rage and shadows fall,
In ever-present love, we stand tall.
For in this bond, we find our place,
A quiet strength, a warm embrace.

Threads of Trust

In woven tales, our secrets lie,
Each thread a bond that won't say goodbye.
We stitch our hopes with gentle hands,
Creating warmth, where love withstands.

Through trials faced and laughter shared,
We build a fortress of love declared.
Each whispered word, a sacred vow,
In threads of trust, we weave our now.

With every choice, the fabric grows,
In patterns rich, our journey flows.
In darkest hours, we'll find our way,
As threads of trust guide us each day.

The tapestry of hearts entwined,
In colors bright, our spirits shine.
For in this weave, our lives are spun,
Together strong, forever one.

So hold me close, don't let me go,
In threads of trust, we'll always glow.
Through every storm, through every test,
With love as thread, we are truly blessed.

Beneath the Surface

A quiet depth lies underneath,
Where dreams and worries intertwine,
In whispers soft, the heart can speak,
Eclipsed by doubt, yet still divine.

With every wave, we dive anew,
Unraveling thoughts, a hidden truth.
In stillness found, our spirits dance,
Beneath the surface, holds romance.

Each breath a ripple, each thought a spark,
Echoes of love in shadows dark.
We navigate this ocean vast,
With every trust, we heal the past.

For in the depths, we find our way,
Embracing light, come what may.
A treasure waits in waters clear,
Beneath the surface, love draws near.

So let us dive, explore the sea,
Hand in hand, just you and me.
In depths uncharted, we'll reside,
Beneath the surface, side by side.

The Warmth Between Us

In every glance, a fire ignites,
A warmth that dances, held so tight.
With gentle smiles, our spirits meet,
In tender moments, love's heartbeat.

As sun-kissed days and moonlit nights,
Illuminate the path of our sights.
With every laugh, the bond grows strong,
In harmony where we belong.

The world around fades in the glow,
Of cherished dreams that softly flow.
In every hug, a realm of trust,
The warmth between us, pure and just.

Through storms that rage and winds that sway,
The warmth will guide us on our way.
In every heartbeat, every sigh,
A flame eternal, you and I.

So let us bask in love's embrace,
In every moment, find our place.
For in this warmth, we shine so bright,
The warmth between us, pure delight.

Whispers of Solace

In twilight's embrace, whispers roam,
Soft echoes dance, calling us home.
Each breath a comfort, tender and light,
Guiding our souls through the quiet night.

Beneath the stars, dreams gently weave,
A tapestry of hope, hearts believe.
Through silent wishes, the moon imparts,
The soothing balm to our restless hearts.

In every sigh, a story unfolds,
Of love and courage, in whispers told.
As shadows fade, the dawn will rise,
Bringing with it, the brightest skies.

In nature's arms, we find our place,
Embracing the stillness, a gentle grace.
The world around, a soft lullaby,
Cradling our spirits as time slips by.

Whispers of solace, a healing flow,
In moments shared, together we grow.
Through every sorrow, joy we ignite,
Hand in hand, we shine our light.

Embrace of a Gentle Heart

With every heartbeat, love takes flight,
In the quiet folds of the starry night.
Gentle whispers wrapped in grace,
Finding warmth in a sweet embrace.

Through life's storms, we hold on tight,
Finding strength in the softest light.
With open arms, like the skies above,
The world feels right when it's filled with love.

In laughter shared and tears that fall,
A bond so deep, it conquers all.
With every heartbeat, our spirits align,
Creating a rhythm, forever divine.

In the valley of dreams, we rise and soar,
A dance of souls forevermore.
Together we journey, hand in hand,
In this embrace, we perfectly stand.

With every step, our stories entwine,
In the garden of hope, brightly we shine.
The embrace of a gentle heart reveals,
The love that nurtures, the truth it feels.

In Shadows and Light

Within the shadows, the mysteries hide,
Unseen whispers that drift with the tide.
In gentle glimmers, the truth will gleam,
A tapestry woven from each dream.

Through the veil of night, we dare to seek,
The light in the silence, the strength in the meek.
Each step a journey, each breath a chance,
To dance with the shadows in twilight's trance.

In the balance of dusk, where two worlds meet,
The heart finds solace, a rhythm, a beat.
Through valleys deep and mountains high,
With courage bold, we learn to fly.

In the embrace of dusk, we let go fears,
Finding beauty that sparkles through all the years.
In shadows and light, we carve our way,
With love as our compass, guiding our stay.

The harmony sings of both dark and bright,
In shadows and light, we find our sight.
Together we walk, through thick and thin,
In every heart's whisper, the journey begins.

A Friend in the Silence

In quiet corners, where shadows play,
A friend awaits, in her soft array.
With gentle eyes, she reads the soul,
Her silent wisdom, making us whole.

In moments shared, where words can flee,
Understanding blooms like a timeless tree.
With every glance, a story speaks,
In laughter's echo, in solace it leaks.

Through seasons changing, hand in hand,
We weave our tales, a friendship so grand.
In silence, we find a sacred space,
A bond not bound by time or place.

In whispered dreams, our hopes ignite,
With every heartbeat, love takes flight.
In the stillness, her spirit shines,
A friend in the silence, where love entwines.

With open hearts, we cherish the bond,
In laughter and tears, forever we're fond.
A friend in silence, a treasure rare,
In every moment, a love we share.

Threads of Connection

In the quiet corners, shadows meet,
Whispers of laughter, feel the heartbeat.
A glance exchanged, a knowing smile,
Threads of connection weave all the while.

Bonds like the stars, shining bright,
Guiding us home through the dark of night.
With every story, a tapestry grows,
In the depths of our hearts, the truth flows.

The world spins on, yet we stand still,
Embraced by warmth, by our shared will.
In moments fleeting, we find our place,
A dance of souls, a sacred space.

Time may unravel, but we'll restore,
The ties that bind us, forevermore.
Through trials faced, through joy and pain,
Connection lingers, like autumn rain.

So hold me close, let silence speak,
In our togetherness, we're strong, not weak.
For in the weave of every day,
We find the love that will never stray.

The Heart's Sanctuary

Within the silence, a refuge lies,
Where dreams take flight and spirit flies.
In sacred corners, peace unfolds,
The heart's sanctuary, quiet and bold.

Shadows dance with a gentle glow,
Embracing whispers only we know.
Moments of stillness, soft and clear,
Wrap us in warmth, in love sincere.

Memories linger, both old and new,
Carried on breezes, rich and true.
In this haven, we find our grace,
A tranquil garden, a sacred space.

Every heartbeat, a gentle sigh,
In the heart's sanctuary, we learn to fly.
With every breath, we release the pain,
And gather strength like summer rain.

So let the world fade, let worries cease,
In this safe haven, we find true peace.
Together as one, in love's embrace,
We build a fortress, a timeless place.

Echoes of Solace

In the hush of twilight, whispers call,
Echoes of solace, soft and small.
A chorus of memories, sweet refrain,
Wanders the earth, kissed by rain.

In shadows deep, we find our way,
Through trials faced in the light of day.
Each step forward, a promise made,
With echoes of comfort, never to fade.

The night sings low, a soothing tune,
In the embrace of the silver moon.
Each heartbeat resonates in our chest,
Easing our burdens, granting us rest.

Life's fleeting moments, like stars align,
In the echoes of solace, everything's fine.
Through pain and laughter, joy and strife,
The echoes remind us of the beauty of life.

So let us linger, let silence reign,
In the gentle whispers, release the pain.
For in the echoes, we find our calm,
A balm for the soul, a healing psalm.

The Power of Presence

In stillness shared, we find our might,
The power of presence, a guiding light.
A touch, a gaze, speaks louder than words,
In the quiet moments, comfort is heard.

With every heartbeat, a world we build,
In the space between us, dreams are fulfilled.
No need for grand gestures, the loud and clear,
Just being together, all we hold dear.

In laughter and tears, we dance as one,
Through valleys of doubt, we rise with the sun.
The essence of love, a steady embrace,
In the power of presence, we find our place.

So linger a while, let the moments align,
In the tapestry woven, your heart is mine.
Simple and true, in connection we trust,
The threads of our beings, in unity, must.

For in every gaze, in every shared breath,
We celebrate life, conquer the depths.
With the power of presence, we heal and grow,
A gift everlasting, the love that we sow.

Unwavering Support

In shadows deep, you stand by me,
A lighthouse bright, eyes keen and free.
Through storms that rage and winds that bite,
Your steady hand brings warmth and light.

With every doubt, you calm my fears,
A steady heart, you've shared my tears.
In silence bold, your strength unfolds,
A bond unbreakable, worth more than gold.

Through valleys low and mountains high,
Together strong, we learn to fly.
Your faith in me, a gentle guide,
In every moment, you're by my side.

No matter where this path may lead,
Your heart is where I plant my seed.
In laughter's light and sorrow's shade,
A trust so deep, it won't ever fade.

You see my dreams, you hear my cries,
With open arms, you lift me high.
In the dance of life, a perfect pair,
Unwavering support beyond compare.

Voices of Serendipity

Whispers weave through the softest night,
Unexpected paths take their flight.
In chance encounters, fate aligns,
With every step, new joy entwines.

The laughter shared, a fleeting spark,
In strangers' smiles, we leave a mark.
In gentle words, the magic flows,
Unraveled tales where friendship grows.

Moments linger like fragrant air,
In serendipity's sweet snare.
Each twist of fate, a song to sing,
In harmony, the heart takes wing.

From quiet corners, secrets bloom,
In tender glances, dispelling gloom.
The universe hums a tune so bright,
Voices unite in pure delight.

Embrace the chance, let life unfold,
In every story, a treasure told.
Through laughter's echo, we find our way,
In serendipity, we choose to stay.

Lighthouses in the Fog

A beacon shines through swirling haze,
Guiding lost souls through shadowed ways.
In every flash, a hope ignites,
Lighthouses stand through darkest nights.

As waves crash down on rocky shores,
These steadfast towers sing their scores.
With every beam, a promise made,
That love and light will never fade.

Through whispers soft and fears that climb,
Each guiding light defies all time.
In moments dim, they stand as one,
Their hearts ablaze till day is done.

When fog descends and pathways blur,
Their steady voices gently stir.
With courage bold and spirits bright,
Lighthouses pierce the shrouded night.

Together bound, we find our way,
With candles lit, we'll never sway.
In unity, our strength prevails,
Through love's embrace, we sail our sails.

Gentle Embrace

In whispered tones, the world feels right,
A gentle breeze, a soft twilight.
Arms that cradle, warm and near,
In every hug, an end to fear.

With tender love, we share our dreams,
In quiet moments, serenity beams.
Together wrapped in trust divine,
A gentle embrace, your heart in mine.

Through trials faced and mountains climbed,
In every challenge, we've intertwined.
No tempest strong can tear apart,
This gentle bond, a work of art.

When weary days begin to fade,
A loving touch where hope is laid.
The world outside may spin and race,
Yet here we find our sacred space.

In laughter's glow and silence sweet,
You make my journey feel complete.
With every heartbeat, we ignite,
A gentle love, our guiding light.

Flames of Friendship

In laughter bright, we gather near,
Our hopes and dreams, we hold so dear.
Through stormy nights and sunny days,
A bond ignites in myriad ways.

With whispered secrets shared at night,
We chase away the creeping fright.
In every tear, in every smile,
We walk together, mile by mile.

Through trials faced and battles won,
A flame burns bright, a love begun.
In quiet moments, hearts entwine,
Forevermore, your hand in mine.

As seasons change and years go by,
We'll light the path, just you and I.
So let us cherish every chance,
For in this life, we share our dance.

In twilight's glow, our shadows blend,
A testament of love, my friend.
Together forged, we'll never break,
In flames of friendship, hearts awake.

Bonds of Benevolence

A simple act, a gentle smile,
We carve our path with love worthwhile.
In kindness shared, we find our way,
Each tiny gesture, brightens the day.

With open hearts, we lend our hands,
In whispered hopes, a bond still stands.
Through trials faced and laughter, too,
Together we will see it through.

Compassion flows like rivers run,
In giving freely, we have won.
For in the heart, true wealth we see,
Bonds of benevolence set us free.

Each story told, each burden shared,
In every moment, love is bared.
Through thick and thin, we hold the line,
In this brave world, our hearts align.

So let us sow the seeds of grace,
In every heart, a sacred space.
With every step, our voices blend,
In bonds of benevolence, we mend.

The Unbroken Circle

In every heart, a sacred tie,
An unbroken circle, you and I.
Through trials thick and joys we share,
Together always, love laid bare.

With every smile and every tear,
In silence deep, we still are near.
The paths we walk, forever bound,
In every memory, love profound.

Through every storm, we find our way,
An unbroken bond, come what may.
In whispered words, our secrets flow,
In endless trust, together grow.

So take my hand, we'll face the sun,
In unity our hearts are one.
The circle spins, time cannot sever,
In love's embrace, we live forever.

In every moment shared, we shine,
An unbroken circle, yours and mine.
Through ups and downs, we will not fall,
In love's embrace, we'll conquer all.

Light in the Gloom

In shadows deep, where fears reside,
We search for hope, our hearts our guide.
A flicker dim, but still it glows,
A light in the gloom, a love that grows.

With every step through darkened days,
We weave a path in shifting ways.
In quiet whispers, warmth we find,
Together facing what's maligned.

As stars above break through the night,
We chase away the creeping fright.
For in the dark, our dreams ignite,
A beacon bright, forever light.

In every tear, a silver line,
Amidst the gloom, our spirits shine.
Each moment shared, a sacred spell,
In unity, we rise and dwell.

So take my hand when hope feels thin,
We'll forge ahead, together win.
In darkest nights, our hearts will bloom,
Together strong, light in the gloom.

The Gift of Togetherness

In laughter shared under the sun,
Hearts intertwined, as one we run.
Through trials faced, hand in hand,
Stronger together, we boldly stand.

In quiet moments, a glance or two,
Words unspoken, yet deeply true.
The warmth we bring in every embrace,
Together we find our rightful place.

Through storms that rage and winds that howl,
Side by side, we make our vow.
In joy and sorrow, our spirits unite,
In the gift of togetherness, we find our light.

With memories cherished, our story unfolds,
In the fabric of life, our journey bold.
Each thread a moment, each stitch a laugh,
Together we craft our colorful path.

As seasons change and years drift by,
Our bond grows deeper, reaching the sky.
In the dance of life, with you I sway,
In togetherness, we find our way.

Unseen Threads

In silence, we weave our dreams at night,
Invisible threads, shining bright.
A gentle pull, a whispered song,
Binding us close, where we belong.

Through bustling streets and quiet nooks,
Connection blooms, like well-read books.
A knowing glance as paths entwine,
Unseen threads, forever align.

In crowded rooms, a peaceful space,
Hearts recognize a familiar face.
Across the miles, the feelings grow,
A tapestry of love, we sew.

When shadows loom and doubts arise,
The threads sustain, beneath the skies.
We hold each other, though far apart,
In unseen bonds, we share one heart.

So let's cherish the ties that bind,
In every moment, kindness we find.
Through life's great weave, let's boldly thread,
Our stories intertwine, in love we're fed.

Comfort's Song

In soft whispers, the night descends,
Comfort settles as the day ends.
In velvet shadows, we softly sway,
Cradled in warmth, we find our way.

With open arms, we welcome peace,
In tender moments, our worries cease.
A melody hums, sweet and low,
Comfort's song, a gentle flow.

Through trials faced and fears released,
In simple joys, we find our feast.
In every heartbeat, a soothing balm,
Together we breathe, together we calm.

In cozy corners, where stories blend,
Reminders of love, as moments send.
Wrapped in a blanket, side by side,
In comfort's song, we take our stride.

As dawn approaches, the light will rise,
Through comforting whispers, the spirit flies.
With hearts united, our souls belong,
In each embrace, we hear comfort's song.

Tales from the Heart

In every heart, a story waits,
Whispers of love, of opened gates.
Through laughter and tears, the truth we seek,
Tales from the heart, where spirits speak.

From childhood dreams to hope's embrace,
Every chapter full of grace.
In the pages turned, memories gleam,
Together we weave the fabric of dreams.

In moments shared, we find our way,
With cherished friends, come what may.
In the tale of us, through thick and thin,
The journey unfolds, where love begins.

With each sunset, a new tale spins,
In every ending, a fresh start begins.
The heart holds on to lessons learned,
In every beat, our passion burns.

Through time and distance, we'll always find,
The tales from the heart, forever entwined.
A story of life, rich and bright,
In the depths of the heart, we find our light.

A Bridge of Comfort

In shadows deep, we find our grace,
A gentle touch, a warm embrace.
Together we walk this winding road,
Finding solace, lightening the load.

With each step shared, our hearts align,
Through whispered words, like aged wine.
A bridge we build with love and care,
In every moment, we find repair.

When storms arise and skies turn gray,
Your hand in mine will lead the way.
Through trials faced and fears laid bare,
A bridge of comfort, forever there.

In laughter shared and tears released,
We forge connections, love increased.
A bond so strong, it won't decay,
Through time and space, come what may.

So let us cherish this sacred thread,
With open hearts, where we are led.
In unity, we rise above,
A bridge of comfort, built on love.

In the Light of Care

Beneath the stars, where quiet flows,
A whisper soft, the heart bestows.
In the light of care, we find our way,
With gentle hands, we mold the clay.

Each moment shared, a spark ignites,
Illuminating darkest nights.
Through trials faced in softest grace,
In the light of care, we find our place.

With open eyes and listening hearts,
We gather strength as love imparts.
A beacon bright in tempest's shroud,
In the light of care, standing proud.

Together we weave a tapestry fine,
Threaded in kindness, pure and divine.
In laughter and tears, we grow and share,
A radiant gift, this light of care.

As time unfolds and seasons change,
Our bond remains, unbound, unstrange.
Forever nurtured, our souls declare,
In this embrace, the light of care.

Echoes of Empathy

In every heart, a story dwells,
An echo soft, where silence swells.
Through eyes that mirror, feelings blend,
Echoes of empathy, love will send.

Beyond the words, a deeper sense,
A silent pact, a shared defense.
In moments fragile, hearts will mend,
Through echoes of empathy, we transcend.

A gentle nod, a knowing glance,
In unity, we find our chance.
Together we rise through joy and pain,
Echoes of empathy's sweet refrain.

With every heartbeat, every sigh,
We honor voices that never die.
In this embrace, our spirits blend,
Echoes of empathy, a timeless trend.

So let us listen and open wide,
The door to understanding, side by side.
In every story, every end,
Echoes of empathy shall extend.

Harmony in Presence

In stillness found, beneath the trees,
The world slows down, we catch the breeze.
With each breath drawn, a song is played,
Harmony in presence, softly laid.

With open hearts, we gather close,
In shared stillness, our spirits boast.
The beauty lies in moments rare,
In harmony of presence, love laid bare.

Through laughter shared and silence felt,
In sacred space, our worries melt.
Together we walk, in gentle care,
Finding refuge in harmony rare.

In this embrace, time fades away,
A dance of souls, come what may.
United we stand, with joy to share,
In harmony of presence, hearts laid bare.

As dusk approaches, stars ignite,
Our bond shines bright, a guiding light.
Forever cherished, moments we dare,
In harmony of presence, a love so rare.

Shelter from Storms

Under the roof, we gather close,
Whispers of safety, a cherished prose.
Raindrops tap against the wood,
Here in the warmth, all feels good.

Lightning flickers, a brief display,
We share our secrets, come what may.
The world's wild chaos fades away,
In this haven, we choose to stay.

Outside, the winds rage and howl,
But inside, peace wears a gentle cowl.
With every heartbeat, a gentle song,
In shelter's embrace, we all belong.

A cozy quilt wraps us tight,
Stories unfold in the soft light.
Together we weave a tapestry bright,
Finding joy in the tempest's fight.

This bond we forge, strong and true,
In storms, we know just what to do.
With laughter and love, our spirits soar,
In this shelter forevermore.

A Dance of Souls

Under moonlight, shadows sway,
Hearts entwined in the night's ballet.
Each step whispers, a silent sigh,
As stars twinkle in the sky.

A gentle twirl, a fleeting glance,
In that moment, we start to dance.
The world outside fades away,
In this rhythm, we choose to stay.

With every turn, we break the mold,
Stories of dreams and memories told.
In the soft glow, time stands still,
Lost in the music, a shared thrill.

Together we move, like the tide,
In this dance, there's nothing to hide.
Two souls spark in a cosmic scene,
In the sweet silence, we reign supreme.

As dawn approaches, we hold on tight,
Knowing this dance lit up the night.
In every heartbeat, a promise unfolds,
A dance of souls, forever bold.

Moments of Connection

In fleeting glances, worlds collide,
A spark ignites, hearts open wide.
In a crowded room, we find our space,
In silence shared, a warm embrace.

Words unspoken, yet understood,
A bond that's formed, as it should.
In laughter shared, joy resonates,
Each moment cherished, no room for fates.

Paths may cross, then drift apart,
But in our veins, there's a shared heart.
In brief encounters, truths are born,
In the tapestry of life, love is worn.

Finding solace in a stranger's smile,
For just a moment, we walk a mile.
No need for plans, just here and now,
Together, we take a joint vow.

In this fleeting dance, we reconnect,
A universe vast, we both reflect.
Moments of beauty in every glance,
Life's sweetest gift, our shared chance.

Soft Footsteps

In the quiet night, footsteps trace,
A gentle rhythm, a peaceful grace.
Echoes linger where shadows play,
Soft as whispers, they drift away.

Through moonlit paths, calm is the air,
Each step forward, without a care.
The world is still, the night is young,
Every heartbeat, a song unsung.

Underneath the stars, secrets unfold,
Stories and dreams, softly told.
With every footfall, life's sweet flow,
In these quiet moments, we learn to grow.

The beauty of dusk paints the town,
With soft footsteps, we journey down.
In the fabric of night, peace we seek,
Every soft whisper makes us weak.

Together we walk, together we breathe,
In this serene dance, we gently weave.
Finding solace in each other's stride,
In soft footsteps, love will abide.

The Language of Kindness

A gentle word can heal the heart,
It builds a bridge, a work of art.
Compassion shines through simple deeds,
Planting softly, love's true seeds.

In every smile, a warmth we share,
An embrace, a moment, a breath of care.
Kindness blossoms, bright and true,
Creating light in all we do.

When storms arise and shadows fall,
Kind words can conquer, long and tall.
Through trials faced with open hands,
Together, united, kindness stands.

It speaks in gestures, loud and clear,
In whispered hopes, it draws us near.
The language rich with silent grace,
In kindness found, we find our place.

So let us weave with tender thread,
A tapestry for hearts we spread.
In every corner, let love find,
The beauty held in kindness defined.

Pillars of Strength

Through trials faced, we stand as one,
In darkest hours, our fears we shun.
Like sturdy oaks, we rise and bend,
With roots that anchor, never end.

In each setback, we learn to grow,
With every challenge, our courage shows.
United voices, bold and clear,
Through whispered doubts, we persevere.

Support like branches, reaching high,
Together we soar, we will not die.
Each pillar strong, a steadfast friend,
In love and hope, our strength transcends.

The burdens shared, the laughter spread,
Together, forging paths we tread.
Through storms and winds, we will not break,
In every heartbeat, bonds we make.

So let us stand, hand in hand tight,
In shadows dark, we'll find the light.
As pillars raised, we journey on,
With every step, our fears are gone.

A Symphony of Souls

In harmony, our spirits dance,
With every heartbeat, every chance.
Together weaving woven sounds,
The love that lifts, the joy that bounds.

Each note a thread, a story told,
In melodies both bright and bold.
Voices rise, a chorus sweet,
In unity, our hearts will meet.

The rhythm flows, a gentle tide,
Together, side by side we glide.
In every silence, echoes play,
A symphony that lights the way.

With every chord that fills the air,
We find our strength, we banish care.
As instruments of love we stand,
Creating magic, hand in hand.

So let us play this song of grace,
In every heart, find our place.
In this grand symphony we know,
Connected deeply, love will grow.

The Art of Listening

In quietude, the heart can hear,
A whispered thought, a hidden tear.
With open ears and minds so clear,
The art of listening draws us near.

Each story shared, a world untold,
In gentle tones, we slowly unfold.
With patience wrapped in kindness' glow,
The heart learns wisdom in ebb and flow.

Through silence deep, we find our ground,
In every pause, connection found.
A nod, a smile, the spark of trust,
In listening, we find the must.

So shut the noise, take time to be,
To truly hear what's meant to free.
For in each word, a truth awaits,
The art of listening opens gates.

Let's wander through this sacred space,
In every story, time and grace.
With hearts attuned, let's shine our light,
In the art of listening, love ignites.

Gentle Hearts

In whispers soft, they speak their truth,
Two souls entwined, reclaiming youth.
With every glance, a tale unfolds,
In gentle hearts, love brightly holds.

They walk through storms, hand in hand,
In quiet strength, together they stand.
With laughter shared and dreams anew,
Each moment cherished, just me and you.

The world may rush, but they move slow,
In sacred spaces, their love can grow.
With tender words, they light the night,
In gentle hearts, everything feels right.

Through trials faced, they find their way,
In every challenge, love will stay.
A bond that's forged in trust and grace,
In gentle hearts, they find their place.

Under starlit skies, they dream as one,
With hopes and wishes, the night begun.
With hands entwined, they set their sights,
On gentle hearts and endless nights.

Beneath the Kindness

Where shadows fall, a light does glow,
In acts of love, our spirits grow.
For every heart that dares to care,
Beneath the kindness, hope lays bare.

A simple smile, a helping hand,
In woven threads, together we stand.
Through struggles faced, we lift each other,
In this embrace, we reveal our mother.

The world may weigh with heavy chains,
But kindness brightens all our gains.
In gentle words, despair takes flight,
Beneath the kindness, we find our light.

In moments rare, when hearts beat strong,
We gather close, where we belong.
For every tear, a joy unfolds,
Beneath the kindness, love's story told.

As seasons change, may we inspire,
With open hearts, we blaze a fire.
Each act we share, a sacred ground,
Beneath the kindness, peace is found.

A Hand to Hold

In darkest nights, when fears arise,
A hand to hold, a strength that ties.
Through trials faced and paths unplanned,
Together we rise, hand in hand.

With gentle touch, we calm the storm,
In silent vows, our souls keep warm.
Through winding roads, we find our way,
A hand to hold, come what may.

Where burdens lie, we share the load,
In every turn, our love bestowed.
With laughter bright, we light the way,
A hand to hold, in night or day.

The journey long, but never alone,
In whispered dreams, our hearts have grown.
In every challenge, our spirits mold,
A hand to hold, as stories unfold.

In tender moments, love speaks loud,
With every heartbeat, we feel proud.
Through thick and thin, our love is bold,
A hand to hold, a tale retold.

In Silent Support

When words escape, and silence reigns,
In quiet strength, compassion gains.
For every struggle that we face,
In silent support, we find our space.

With gentle eyes, we see the pain,
In soft embraces, light remains.
Through unspoken ties, our hearts align,
In silent support, love will shine.

A listening ear, an open heart,
In shared moments, we play our part.
Together we stand, though storms may break,
In silent support, we mend and make.

With every sigh, we lift the weight,
In patient trust, we cultivate.
In darkness faced, our spirits soar,
In silent support, we offer more.

As seasons shift, and days go by,
In quietude, our souls reply.
With love unspoken, but always true,
In silent support, I stand with you.

Trails of Understanding

In shadows cast by thoughts untold,
We wander paths of truths unfold.
With every step, we seek the light,
Embracing all, from day to night.

With voices soft, we start to share,
The stories carved from silent air.
Each moment holds a lesson's grace,
And wisdom blooms in every space.

Through tangled roots and winding ways,
We learn to dance through life's complex maze.
In unity, we find our song,
Together, where we all belong.

As we explore the human heart,
In every bond, we play our part.
Compassion guides us, hand in hand,
Creating peace across the land.

So let us tread this trail with care,
In understanding, love we'll share.
With open hearts, we rise above,
Forging paths of hope and love.

The Strength of the Heart

In battles fought with silent grace,
The heart unveils its sacred space.
With every beat, we stand so tall,
In love's embrace, we never fall.

Through storms that rage and trials faced,
The heart remains, forever braced.
For in its core, resilience lies,
A testament that never dies.

With gentle rhythm, soft and true,
It carves the paths we wander through.
In moments dark and shadows cast,
The strength of love will always last.

Supported by a cherished thread,
Through every tear, and words unsaid.
In unity, we find our might,
Together, we ignite the light.

So celebrate this beating sound,
In every heart, true strength is found.
With courage fierce, we rise anew,
In love's embrace, we find what's true.

A Pause for Kindness

In fleeting moments, still and bright,
We find the strength to do what's right.
With open hearts and gentle hands,
We weave the threads of lifetime's strands.

A smile exchanged, a helping hand,
In kindness shared, we understand.
Each act of grace, a seed we sow,
In tender ways, our love will grow.

For in this world, so fast, we race,
A pause for kindness finds its place.
With every gesture, large or small,
We build the bridges, break the walls.

So let us stop and take a breath,
In kindness' light, we conquer death.
For when we pause and simply care,
We find the magic waiting there.

With every heartbeat, every breath,
The power lies beyond mere depth.
A pause for kindness shines so bright,
In shared humanity, we ignite.

Reflections of Love

In every glance, a story's spun,
A dance of souls, forever one.
Through whispered dreams and laughter shared,
In love's embrace, we feel prepared.

Like morning dew on petals bright,
Love's gentle touch ignites the night.
Each heartbeat echoes, soft and clear,
In every memory we hold dear.

The stars align when two hearts meet,
In tender moments, pure and sweet.
Through every trial, hand in hand,
Together, we will always stand.

In mirrored eyes, we find our truth,
Reflecting dreams that burst with youth.
Each love story, a sacred thread,
In every word, our spirits fed.

So let love guide us, strong and free,
In every heartbeat's melody.
Reflections glow in joy's embrace,
Two souls entwined in boundless grace.